D0753180

CHICKENS

BY CYNTHIA AMOROSO AND BOB NOYED

PUBLISHED BY THE CHILD'S WORLD®

Published by The Child's World®
1980 Lookout Drive • Mankato, MN 56003-1705
800-599-READ • www.childsworld.com

ACKNOWLEDGMENTS
The Child's World®: Mary Swensen, Publishing Director
The Design Lab: Design
Michael Miller: Editing
Sarah M. Miller: Editing

DESIGN ELEMENTS
© Doremi/Shutterstock.com

PHOTO CREDITS
© dima266f/Bigstockphoto.com: 9; dragang/Bigstockphoto.com:
14-15; J Parker/Shutterstock.com: 18; kaarsten/Bigstockphoto.
com: 6; kay roxby/Shutterstock.com: 17; khunaspix/Bigstockphoto.
com: 10; monticello/Bigstockphoto.com: 5; nimnull/Bigstockphoto.
com: cover; paulbroad/Bigstockphoto.com: 12; Thomas Zobl/
Shutterstock.com: 20-21; Volff/Bigstockphoto.com: 19

ISBN: 9781503808249
LCCN: 2015958465

Printed in the United States of America
Mankato, MN
June, 2016
PA02308

Table of Contents

Clucking Hens

Chickens are birds that many people raise on farms. Chickens make funny sounds. Female chickens are called **hens**. Hens make a "cluck, cluck" sound.

DID YOU KNOW?

CHICKENS WEIGH BETWEEN 5 AND 7 POUNDS (2 AND 3 KILOGRAMS).

Chicks

Baby chickens are called **chicks**. They hatch from eggs. Chicks have soft, fuzzy feathers. They make a "cheep, cheep" sound.

Roosters

Male chickens are called **roosters**. They have bright feathers. Roosters say "cock-a-doodle-doo."

DID YOU KNOW?
ROOSTERS HAVE SPURS ON THE BACKS OF THEIR LEGS.

Chicken Bodies

Chickens are covered with feathers. Chickens have a beak, two legs, two wings, and a tail.

DID YOU KNOW?

THE COMB AND WATTLE KEEP A CHICKEN
COOL IN HOT WEATHER.

Combs and Wattles

A chicken looks as if it is wearing a red hat. This is called a **comb**.

A chicken also looks as if it has a red beard. This is called a **wattle**.

Colors

There are many colors of chickens. Chickens can be black, white, red, brown, or orange.

DID YOU KNOW?
THERE ARE HUNDREDS OF KINDS OF CHICKENS IN THE WORLD. EACH KIND LOOKS DIFFERENT.

Eating

Chickens eat a lot of food. They eat even when they are not hungry. They like corn, oats, and wheat.

DID YOU KNOW?
CHICKENS WILL ALSO EAT BUGS, WORMS, FRUIT, SEEDS, AND VEGETABLES.

Important Chickens

Farm chickens live in buildings called **coops**. A coop can hold many chickens.

Farmers raise chickens for their
eggs. People also eat the meat
from chickens.

DID YOU KNOW?

CHICKENS CAN LIVE TO BE 5 TO 10 YEARS OLD.

Chickens are important animals. They make funny sounds. We can hear "cluck, cluck," "cheep, cheep," and "cock-a-doodle-doo."

Glossary

CHICKS (CHIKS) Chicks are baby chickens.

COMB (KOHM) A comb is a fleshy piece that sticks up from a chicken's head.

COOPS (KOOPS) Coops are buildings where farm chickens live.

HENS (HENZ) Hens are female chickens.

ROOSTERS (ROO-sturz) Roosters are male chickens.

SPURS (SPURZ) Spurs are sharp spikes on the back of a rooster's legs.

WATTLE (WAT-ull) The fleshy part under a chicken's beak is a wattle.

To Learn More

IN THE LIBRARY

Black, Vickie. *Young Chicken Farmers: Tips for Kids Raising Backyard Chickens*. Edina, MN: Beavers Pond Press, 2013.

Caughey, Melissa. *A Kid's Guide to Keeping Chickens*. North Adams, MA: Storey Publishing, 2015.

Gibbons, Gail. *Chicks & Chickens*. New York, NY: Holiday House, 2005.

ON THE WEB

Visit our Web site for links about chickens: **childsworld.com/links**

Note to Parents, Teachers, and Librarians: We routinely verify our Web links to make sure they are safe and active sites. So encourage your readers to check them out!

23

Index

ABOUT THE AUTHORS

Cynthia Amoroso is an assistant superintendent in a Minnesota school district. She enjoys reading, writing, gardening, traveling, and spending time with friends and family.

Bob Noyed has worked in school communications and public relations. He continues to write for both children and adult audiences. Bob lives in Woodbury, Minnesota.